Healing the
World

First Published June 2009

© Copyright,

The White Eagle Publishing Trust, 2009

ISBN 978-0-85487-207-7

Chapter decorations by Rosemary Young

Printed and bound in Sri Lanka
by Printcare Universal (Pvt) Ltd.

Healing the World

WHITE EAGLE

The world needs healing and it needs you!

The White Eagle Publishing Trust

New Lands : Liss : Hampshire : England

*A selection of other books by White Eagle is
shown at the end of this volume.*

CONTENTS

Introduction

In the classic 'HEAL THYSELF' White Eagle tells us that 'All men and women can be servers, healers. To be a servant of God is the most lovely opportunity given to you.' The much-loved book takes the reader on a spiritual path towards a life which is mentally and spiritually healthy, a life that achieves healing through inner peace and self-mastery, and leads us to a state of physical harmony, ultimately bringing us to the stage where we are ready to bring healing to the world.

In 'HEALING THE WORLD' White Eagle continues the process of self-healing. Having brought us to the point at which we are ready to become healers, he leads us further along the path

7

of healing; guiding us to become healers of our planet, of each other, and ultimately of ourselves. Through opening ourselves to the healing power of spirit, we are given a unique and beautiful contact with God, finding inner peace and beauty that will bring healing to our lives.

This long-awaited sequel to a popular spiritual classic is both an uplifting read and a working document, in which the reader is led by a spiritual teacher along a path to healing and self-discovery. It opens where HEAL THYSELF ended – at a healing service – and gives a clear spiritual message: The world needs healing – and it needs you.

White Eagle's teaching is very simple, and it is also very profound. You may find that you are drawn back to the words in this book again and again, and that each time you read them, they seem to mean something new. We hope that they lead you on the path to a beautiful and personal healing.

Notes on the Text

There are some passages of White Eagle's teaching included in this new book which have been printed as extracts in other White Eagle books. They have been included in this compilation in order to give a more complete picture of the overall theme of 'Healing the World'.

Definitions of Terms White Eagle Uses

The Master

There are many references in this book and others to 'the Master', or 'your Master'. White Eagle is not referring to any one particular external teacher. The reader can choose to identify with a known teacher, such as Jesus, or with the inner Master, the Christ within.

It is also important to note that there is no gender associated with this term. Illumined teachers are both masculine and feminine. White Eagle also speaks of brotherhood, or the Brotherhood in spirit, in a way which is not intended to limit it to either sex.

Jesus the Christ

White Eagle distinguishes between the man Jesus (a Master and teacher) and the Christ which is the son/daughter of God and the light which shines in every human heart to a greater or lesser degree. All masters, saints and great teachers have been illumined by this light.

The Star

A six-pointed Star (shining with this Christ light) is a powerful symbol which White Eagle has given for use in all his healing work. It is composed of two equilateral triangles, superimposed without divisions, symbolising a human being totally illumined by the Christ light. This in itself is a symbol of a master soul. Visualising this symbol shining upon the world, an individual, an animal or a condition in need of healing is a powerful aid to healing.

The Star has intrinsic spiritual magic as it actually 'stimulates the Christ light within every heart; thus' it promotes self-healing.

The Star Brotherhood

This is the term White Eagle uses for a heavenly group of illumined souls working 'under the ray of the Star' to heal the world. At the earthly level, in the organisation of the White Eagle Lodge, there is opportunity for those drawn to do so, to make a spiritual commitment of service in the Brotherhood group which was established in 1934 (two years before the actual start of 'the Lodge'—the outer organisation) and has been working to 'heal the world' ever since.

Biblical Quotations

Quotations from the Bible are taken from the authorized version of 1611 and are shown in italics.

Chapter 4.

'Behold, I make all things new.'

Source: Rev. 21:5

'Thou shalt love the Lord thy God with all thy heart, and with all thy soul, and with all thy mind.'

Source: Matt. 22:37

Chapter 5.

'I and my father are one.'

Source: John 10:30

'Love one another.'

Source: John 15:12

Chapter 6.

'I am the resurrection and the life.'

Source: John 11:25

Invocation:

At a Healing Service

We come into your midst from the world of spirit and we bring with us joy. There is an outpouring of the spirit of love upon you all. Forget if you can the claims of physical matter. Unite with us in spirit and be strong in spirit, be strong in the light. Let the spirit of God rise in you to triumph over all weakness and darkness. This is the wisdom you have come to learn. The purpose of your incarnation is for you to become stronger and stronger in spiritual light and power so that you may bring through into daily life the radiance of your spiritual life.

We know your difficulties; we know how the physical body holds you fast in its grip, and because of this, you suffer fears and pains, disorder of mind and spirit. But try to walk the spiritual path, the path of light. When you can make an inner contact with the true source of your being, try to hold fast to it; then you will triumph over the darkness of physical matter.

You are now in a temple of the Star Brotherhood. The walls of this temple are built of shining, luminous substance, and the illumined brothers of all time are with you. Your awareness of their power is only limited by your lower consciousness. Let that recede; let your full spiritual consciousness take possession of you now, and then the rays of light which bring you life and healing will penetrate and run right through your veins and your whole nervous system. Men and women call sudden healing a miracle, but spiritual healing is the will of God—the will of the master mind operating through matter, operating through you. The joy and the light which is here now is filling your whole being......... Take it with you when you go out into the earthly world. Radiate this light and healing to the whole of life.

I. The Path Of The Healer

If you submit yourself in love to God, He will work through you and you cannot go wrong.

1

In treading the path of spiritual unfoldment you cannot advance without your influence and light affecting the lives of all humanity. With every step forward that you as an individual take, you are assisting all humanity to rise towards the light. Each one of you possesses spiritual gifts, and those spiritual gifts will unfold. All gifts of the spirit can be of the greatest service to humanity, and all gifts of the spirit can be embodied into one word. This word is 'healing'. Healing is of the utmost importance for all who would progress on the path. All gifts of the spirit, whatever they may be, are healing gifts. Once you have made this contact with spirit, if only for a flash, you are henceforth a channel, for you have opened the way for the creative power and light to flow into you. As you aspire in sincerity to God, your light shines in the darkness. As we look into your loving hearts, we see all the little earthly weaknesses and failings falling away, and we from the spirit only see that flame, that divine light and glory which is in the heart of your soul. This is what the angels see. This is also what the Masters dwelling in the fastness of the mountains will see, and there will be an instant contact between you and them. Men and women who pray earnestly to be used in the Master's service are noted, and their progress watched. All of you are under the watchful eyes of a servant of the Master—perhaps even the Master himself. No need to make a great noise, but only to do the work which has been given you. Keep on keeping on; care neither for praise nor for blame; but work for the Master and for the very love of service to the whole of creation.

2

The greatest work that you can do on your earth in this age is to heal. Having offered yourselves in sincerity and faith to the work of God and the Brotherhood, remember that the Great Light is waiting for the human channel through which to flow and the starting point of this work is yourself. Never allow earthly thoughts, the doubts and fears of your lower mind to block the channel for the healing light. Your Master teaches you in a very simple way the rules of brotherhood and you must endeavour to understand and apply these rules to your life. Not of yourself can you heal the sick in mind and body. All you have to do is try to be a humble server. You know the truth of this as well as we can tell you, and you know the power which possesses your heart when you humbly present yourself before the divine presence. Even so, sometimes the human mind doubts and cuts you off, but we assure you it is possible to rise above this limitation of the earthly mind.

A Master knows that he cannot command the forces of the unseen until he has complete command of the forces within himself. Those who would penetrate the mysteries of the universe, and understand the complexities of life and human relationships need not look outwards to set this and that person right; they need to look within, and set their own houses in order. We can only give you principles or signposts and you need to work in the simplest way on each problem as it presents itself to you in your daily life, according to the principles given you. We do not come to relieve you of your opportunities. We come to bring you power, wisdom and love. We of the Brotherhood do not expect more than you can give at your present stage on the path, but everyone can, at given times, seek attunement with the eternal Light, can commune with God, can worship God. If you do this in ways most harmonious to you personally, then you will carry with you the healing light.

3

To those of you who already are, or who wish to be spiritual healers, we would say that the first essential is for you to become attuned to the spirit of Christ, and try to feel the great Light pouring into you. The desire to heal is an important step. We do not say it is the first step, but it is a very important step on the path of light. When a man or woman desires to heal they need first of all to set their vision and heart upon the Great Spirit and all that this term involves—the Great Spirit—God. This is what makes the perfect healer or the perfect man/woman. If God is close to you and you are a healer or a server, you have no need to fear that you will not be used at the right moment. You will be filled and filled and filled with the joy of life, with perfect health and with divine knowledge. Entering a room you carry with you the Christ healing rays. Touch a hand, and you send through that physical body the golden healing rays of Christ. If you are speaking the words of a healing service, those words go forth with a vibration of power and healing. If you are sitting in a group, and you are responding to the vibration of that group, your soul will be quickened. There will go forth from you that divine energy which the angelic powers immediately gather and use as they wing their way to the patient who needs your healing service.

4

It is good to prepare your mind, your soul and your body for the inflow of the divine healing. Pray that you may learn to be the master in the lodge of your own being. You can gradually learn to rule your lodge with love and truth, wisdom and beauty. You have come into this temple, into this life of earth, from above. You have latent within you all the attributes of a master, and only you can open the way for these qualities to rule your lodge. 'How,' we hear your unspoken question, 'How can we serve, how act?' You can learn gradually to become aware of the invisible forces which are playing upon the earth life. You can train your body and your higher vehicles to become consciously aware of this stream of light which finds entrance into your being through the psychic centres. You can learn to be aware of this circulating light stream which can re-vivify and glorify body and soul, and pass from you, directed by your highest self, to heal the sick throughout the world ... the sick in body and mind. The vibrations and the power of the angels and the great spiritual beings work through cleansed and prepared human channels to build heaven into the consciousness of humankind.

5

Be calm, steadfast and peaceful. Try not to become agitated. Be at peace within. Accept things as they come and do not be rushed or overcome by the forces of ignorance. Be steadfast, with a quiet, inner, peaceful and persistent knowing that the Great Architect of the Universe holds the Plan of your life in His hand. Remember always the quiet, pure and true contact within the sanctuary of your own being. Be true to your own self, your own spirit, and in being true to yourself you will be true also to God and the universal Brotherhood. Many people on earth and many sources on the etheric plane will delight in trying to pull you away from that still centre of truth. Do not be pulled; but hold fast to the pure vision of goodness, truth and love. Be watchful and alert and do not be beguiled by false values. It is so easy to slip off the straight path!

Those who would bring peace into the lives of others, who would soothe the troubled breast and offer a word of wisdom, need to learn first to control their own being. We advise you to pray amidst the turmoil of your earthly life, for calmness of mind and heart. Be still. Unless there is stillness within, the angels cannot work for you. This is one of the most difficult conditions to which man placed in the vortex of human life can attain; but we would emphasise the great need there is for all souls who aspire to heal, to learn the secret and the power of a tranquil and serene mind. May this be your daily prayer; and when you have attained to a degree of calmness, you will not find it difficult to love. Earnestly pray to unfold these two qualities: peace and love. Without there is the bustle, turmoil and humanity's noise of the outer plane, so typical of life on earth. But within your sanctuary, create peace and love. In your outer life, in the outer courts, there is inharmony, harshness, noise and disturbing elements. We do understand your individual difficulties; we know how hard it is for you to prevent the impatient 'mob' from invading your inner lodge. But this you have to learn to do; this is your work as a healer. You have to retain the peace and sanctity of the lodge within, and so control the outer court that you can hear the voice of the Great Healer...... This voice is one with the Christ within your own heart. In the heart there may always be peace, stillness and love. Deep within your heart is the silence. This is where you make the link with the infinite and eternal creative force, the healing power. It radiates through your aura, it projects through your hands and through every centre of your body—a radiant gift of healing to the world.

II. The Inner Silence

When you enter a room you carry your healing, or God's healing with you.

1

You will find nothing more beautiful than you can find in your own inner temple. Grow strong in this simple truth. The innermost secret of life is to abide in the place of stillness; in tranquillity of spirit. Do not separate yourself at any time from this power; let it be a living force in you. Remember it is possible to withdraw into the innermost even if you are walking the streets of a great city. You do not need to enter into a quiet place, although it is better to shut away the world when you wish to get into contact with the Infinite. It is possible for the body to perform its duties almost automatically on the outer plane whilst prayer is taking place within. It is wise so to live that at any moment, in any place, you can pray, opening your heart to the great silence, to the Infinite, to eternity, and ask for help. Ask that the principle of love may be expressed through you in your dealings with your fellow men and women. We emphasise the necessity for your loyalty to the inward voice of the spirit, your highest self. If man and woman would only be true and loyal to the light, to the love within the heart, each, as an individual, but better still, in a community, could heal and cleanse the whole of humankind.

2

Reach towards the heavenly light, remembering that you can be a reflector of that light. Look up to the sun-capped mountain range, the golden city, call it the kingdom of heaven if you like! But remember that the kingdom of heaven is not really a far country; the kingdom of heaven is found within yourself. You can make it a far country, or it can become close, a world of infinite beauty within yourself. People find it such a temptation, so much easier, to go here, there, everywhere, rushing to all kinds of place, to the east, to the west, to the north, to the south, in search of a master—and all the time the Master is within, so close, nearer than breathing, closer than hands and feet. This is simple truth.

As you learn to seek for this serenity, this peace, this tranquillity; as you learn in humility to kneel before the communion table, you will find the greatest treasure, the perfect gift, and become a trusted servant of God. Your path is clear: respond at all times to the spirit which is God, your highest purest consciousness of God. As you do so your spirit will become stronger; through your response, through your aspirations, the love and power of the spirit will flow to you unmistakably, enabling you to become not only a healer of bodies, but a healer of souls, a healer of nations, a healer of inharmonious conditions, a healer in every sense of the word. Learn to look not only to the God of the universe, but to that part of God which dwells within your own heart, and is all powerful. When you need help in everyday life seek this God within—a God of virtue, goodness and love, but do not mistake your personal self for pure spirit. The divine Presence will never fail you, because it is all wisdom, all knowledge. When you tune in to that divine Self in meditation you will receive pure and direct guidance through the spirit. If you are true to that centre and the compass swings round it, it draws a perfect circle, and within this circle no true mason can ever err. It does not matter what the market-place is saying; truth lies in that centre in yourself. All happiness, all good health, all peace of mind, comes to you from that centre, the dot within the circle. Your spirit tells you what is the true, the loving action. Be true to the voice of your spirit.

A silence is not only no words: do not depend on words. Strive for the inner realisation of the divine Presence. In the silence you contact reality; and 'silence' does not necessarily mean absence of physical sound. It means the silence of all your vehicles; the silence of the physical when it ceases to intrude; the stillness of the emotions, the stillness of the mental body and the silence of the spirit. In this silence is heard the music of God's voice. The truth that you seek is there; all truth, age-old truth. If you feel a little weary sometimes, will you try to remember that the power of love from the Great Spirit is infinite, and will come to you without fail as you humbly enter into the temple of the heart, within your own inner self. When you feel weary and tired, enter into that inner chamber, the heart sanctuary, and kneel before the golden altar, above which hangs the blazing star. Then you will be refreshed. Weariness will fall from you, and you will feel the power of God flow through you abundantly. You will rise, as on wings of light, into the spheres of heavenly power and peace.

4

In spiritual healing not only your body but your soul and your very life is being worked upon. There is a slow permeation of your soul and body by the Christ spirit, the pure healing power. It will work in your daily life; it will change your outlook; it will guide you to select always the good and the true and the beautiful way of life; it will guide you to be tolerant and forgiving, patient and trustful. All these spiritual attributes will gradually develop in the soul who is faithfully trusting in the higher powers, the God power, to heal. Initiation into the inner mysteries of life comes only after the soul has passed many tests and endured many trials. If you are true to the inner light and give your confidence to God, you can be quite sure that as you tread your path you will be helped in countless ways, not only spiritually but physically and materially as well.

The early Brotherhoods learnt that by developing the inner light in themselves, they were able to give consolation and healing to all who suffered. The Master taught that love is the light which is your armour against the world, against darkness. No darkness can penetrate the shining armour of the light which you have drawn around you by the power of love, and as you meditate under the blazing Star. Walk the spiritual path, the path of light. When you get this inner contact with the true source of your being, hold fast; triumph over the darkness of physical matter. Remember that within you is a power, a beautiful light which if you think about it will radiate from you and be your protection. Try to call upon this inner light, and your own higher self, and allow yourself to be filled with the light of God. Try to let it be for you like a great shining armour of protection. Nothing will touch you, nothing can penetrate that shining armour of light which you can put round yourself by the strength of the spirit within you. Learn that you can call upon your own divine

Presence. It is all powerful and can overcome all enemies, all darkness. Take little notice of passing difficulties and obstacles. Pray only for that great love in your heart which will cause you to feel kind, forgiving and gentle, full of trust in God. When you encounter difficulties in your work, when you feel conflicting forces, do not let them overcome you. Do not attack, but remain very still and calm within. Go into the inner silence. Be still, in the strength of the great light of God.

6

Never mind what happens on the outer plane. Keep your vision on the light of God, for it is by the light of the God within you that you are able to look forward and catch a glimpse of the glorious light rising behind the mountains. When you have seen that, nothing will deter you from pressing forward on the path which leads to that sunlight. You will long with all your being to grow nearer to the eternal Sun, to feel its warmth and comfort and glory. Nothing will matter to you but that you become enfolded in it, so that you, being part of the one eternal life, may hold all life in your heart. Then slowly and imperceptibly the flame within the heart will grow brighter and more powerful. Slowly and imperceptibly will dawn an awareness, a consciousness of the higher worlds in which you live. Slowly and imperceptibly you will begin to feel an at-one-ment with God, and the most perfect happiness, the most satisfying joy which sickness will not touch, which death will not destroy, but only enhance. There will come ever increasing awareness of spirit which will accompany you through the portals of this world into the next, and through the next into the heavenly state of bliss. You will be helped by your guardian angel, the angel of karma, to follow the path of service and renunciation, of sacrifice and love. The peace of heaven will bless and fill you, restoring you to harmony and tranquillity. Let you, the captain, command the boat at all times. Cast out fear— there is nothing to fear when you love God.

III. The Need For Healing

Resign all to divine love, but at the same time project light, project love from yourselves into life, all life.

1

There are periods in the world's progress when it is particularly desirable for the white light to manifest, and your individual effort at the present time is most valuable. Today the great need in the world is for healing —healing the nations, healing the soil, healing and caring for the animal kingdom; bringing to humanity the healing balm of the heaven world, and helping people not only to believe, but also feel, the impetus towards goodness and kindness, one to another, and to all God's creation. The world needs all the positive God-thought that you can project, to heal the sick in body and mind. There is great need for your untiring service, and we ask you to give forth to the world, from the well of truth that is within you, the spirit of peace and love and brotherhood. A mighty power from inner centres of light is being concentrated upon world affairs at this time, but also there is the opposite force at work; always there are the two: positive and negative, the constructive and the disintegrating forces, and it is of vital importance that the balance is kept. Try never to think, 'I am so insignificant, I can do nothing'. Try never to fail in your obligation to think positively, to send forth the light of love and goodwill, and to use every opportunity to do the Master's work.

All the world needs healing, and the great healer of all is love. By your love for each other, for all mankind, for the animal kingdom, for the world of nature, for God, you help in the salvation of this planet. The greater your love, the greater your power to help. So many organisations on earth seek to help in the cause of peace and progress, and all these organisations have their place, for they appeal to the varying mentality of men and women. But there is one common de-nominator – all souls will respond to love. It is so simple, so simple that some may get tired of hear-ing the words, "Love one another…. The kingdom of heaven is within". But this is all, it is the com-pleteness of life – to love, to be love, to become at one with love, to become part of the whole of love. Love radiates light, it heals, it comforts. But it is through constant work and living that this will take place. If you have love in your heart, you are doing God's work. You are God's instruments. Never forget a positive, constructive, unshakable thought of God…… God in everything, God everywhere—God Who has power to restore, to heal and to comfort humankind. We would convey to your hearts the truth of the power of love; but this you can prove for yourselves if you will put into operation the law of love in your own life.

3

You can do your best so to live and behave towards your fellow beings that you are continually, not only building the Christ within yourself, but the conditions to which you will move onward when you leave your physical body. If you would make a practice every night, when you lay yourself down to sleep, of thinking of the world of spirit, the heaven world (not the astral plane, but the heaven world), and in your imagination go into that glorious heaven world, then, we assure you, you would 'plug in' to the Source of infinite power, and awaken in the morning refreshed and full of joy. By continually doing this you will train yourselves to live in the consciousness of God and God's beauty, and the light which is there in the higher world. The way to bring about happiness in the heart is to dwell in the consciousness of God and the harmony of God's world. What good will this do? It will do you, as individuals, tremendous good; but more than this, it will help the whole world. This is because your projection of the Light and of the truth of God's love, will gradually find an entrance into the hearts of men and women on earth who live in confusion and sorrow, and unsatisfied desire. The surest way to happiness is to relinquish desire, to surrender to God's love, to try in every way to obey first the principle of God, which is love.

4

If you wish for good things in the world, if you wish to avoid war and conflict, try to learn to live peace and love and goodwill yourself and help others to do the same. Show the way by example and others will seek to find that something which you are manifesting in your life. Strengthen the spirit within you by daily attuning yourself to the world of light. Be tranquil, and know the peace of God and the joy of life, and you will be helping to raise the vibrations of all life and of the earth it-self. You all have responsibilities of a material and spiritual nature. There are many forms of life looking towards you, towards your life, to help them, just as you look towards the light which shines in the distance. God helps you; you help the lesser forms of life. The nature and animal kingdoms look towards the human for help upon the path of evolution as you look towards the an-gelic. You owe a responsibility to the lesser king-doms; in every thought of love and wisdom you radiate you are helping some younger, perhaps tiny life form upwards towards the light. The heart of the universe beats in rhythmic song in all creation... in the song of the birds, in the per-fume and colour of the flowers, in the wind, in the trees, in the sky and the running water, in the sunshine and in the rain in life and in death. Re-member that you are one with all life, that there is one life-stream running through every form of life on many planes of consciousness. Each human soul is part of this grand universal life beat. May your eyes be opened to all the loveliness of nature. Leave the thoughts of the earth and rise in spirit to the spheres of light. We take you up into the world of light, your real home, the home of the spirit and the soul, and we move amongst our brethren in the heavenly garden. You may meditate on the world of nature, but remember also the heavenly nature, for all growing things on earth receive the life forces from the heaven world. We work with you to stimulate your awareness of this infinite and eternal life, the beauty of the life of God. May the light flood through you to heal the whole world.

5

By loving life, and loving your brethren, you are putting all your strength into the great Light which slowly but surely is bringing humanity back to God. Humanity, your brethren, are suffering in the darkness, through lack of at-one-ment and harmony with the cosmic life. You may reach the heart of humanity so easily and so simply through becoming an instrument of that divine love which was expressed in Jesus the Christ. In thought, word and deed, be gentle, be tender. Remember—it is like dealing with tiny babes when you deal with the hearts of your brethren: you would not handle the Christ babe roughly nor harshly. Every soul carries within his or her heart the Christ babe. Be tender with that babe, and love much. Seek in the stillness and silence to discover the beautiful jewel in your brothers and sisters. When you can do this, you will have no barrier between you. You will know why the Star Brotherhood tell you to love one another and to see good in all. Try to see, not the outer covering, but deep, deep within, the jewel within the lotus. This is the vision that can come to every living soul, and when it comes it brings too the deep peace and joy which is of heaven. In the silence of your own soul, kneel beside the still waters and pray to be able to send forth the healing light of the Son of God, the Christ. Behind you is a power beyond your comprehension, waiting only for its children to be channels. May the channel open wide and the light flood through you to heal the whole world and raise it from death and darkness into everlasting light and glory.

Your task is to be a peacemaker and a light-bearer. Radiate peace in your world and in your own country. All can recognise the spirit within themselves and within their brothers and sisters. All can put on one side earthly standards, and see humanity through the eyes of the spirit. So often humans bow the head and look at the earth instead of looking up to the heavens to see the vision of the spiritual realms, the kingdom of God. Having seen the vision of the kingdom of heaven a man or woman can bring this truth down to earth. Try to eliminate criticism and judgment of your brother; just work from the heart in truth and in love. If you are over-anxious, feeling you are not getting the work that you want to do, feeling that you are overcharged with power and you could do so much more than opportunity is given to you to do, we would remind you that you may not always choose your path. You stand before your Master awaiting his orders. When you are ready, the way will open for you. Wait in trustfulness in the divine love; be sure that your karma and dharma will bring, at the right time, the opportunity that you have earned, an expansion of consciousness for which you long. You may not realise it, but every healer who comes to take part in the healing work, either in individual service or in a group, is being healed themselves. You cannot make contact with this power without receiving your own blessing. You know there is an ancient saying that every labourer is called to the temple to receive due payment for his work. At this moment you are called to the temple in spirit, to a very simple humble temple, and it is here that you receive your payment in a spiritual blessing and healing.

IV. Reflect The Light

The world needs all the positive God-thought that you can project, to heal the sick in body and mind.

1

There are many forms of service in your world, but true service is the service of the spirit. Only when the power of love is behind the service, is it true service to life. '*Behold, I make all things new.*' The divine life within you, the spirit, the light, the love of God, is the 'I', and the 'I' becomes the 'We' when all are blended in perfect love and brotherhood. The greatest service that can be given to any soul on earth, or any soul imprisoned in the spheres of desire, is to help that soul to find the peace of God. You can serve humanity in no better way than this; to be an instrument for the forces of the Light. Remember that God needs man through whom to manifest. Do all you can, not to preach, but to live the gospel, to sow light in darkness, to sow goodness where there is lack of goodness; and through love and 'God-thought' to stimulate the good in your brethren. Do not depend upon this or that person for opportunities to serve; you have only to be yourself. You have only to surrender to God, obey His/Her will and accept this, and immediately you become a server; you are helping the world. There is no limit to the rays of light which can pour through you and extend over the whole earth. You may be unaware that you are already serving mankind. Our friends on earth often ask, 'I so long to serve; why is the path of service not shown to me? In order to serve I need certain teaching and help. Why does this not come to me?' But we say that as long as a soul is expressing God in thought, word and action in a human and happy way, he or she is serving God and mankind, even if unconscious of doing it. There is only one law, one commandment: '*Love the Lord thy God with all thy heart and with all thy soul and with all thy mind*'. Love God first, love all that is good in the world, love all that is good in life. See good in life, love God, love good with all your heart and soul and mind. By so doing, you will re-alise how to also love your neighbour as yourself.

2

You ask, how can you best help humanity? We answer, by seeking wisdom, prompted by the love in your heart; by learning to withhold criticism and condemnation; by seeing only the good seeking for manifestation in humankind. Let your thoughts always be constructive, thoughts of peace and good-will, becoming ever more aware of the dynamic power in silence, in harmony and peace. Thought is exceedingly powerful. All life is the result of thought, and as humans think so they become; as humans think so they create their life and surroundings. This is the secret of happiness, and finding joy in service; if you are tilling the ground, watering the flowers—whatever you are doing, even if you are perhaps weary and unhappy, think to yourself, 'I am doing this for God, not for myself, but for God ... God ... God'. Your thought of God brings healing to your heart, and healing to the particular condition or person you desire to help. Think peace... and be on the alert to obey the voice you hear in the stillness of your heart. Hold fast to courage and the deep faith that the light can never be extinguished.Ever seek the true interpretation of what you see and hear on earth. Continually make an effort to live according to spiritual values. Live, refusing to be entangled or held down by wrong values; and when you see the right, keep to the right and do not be influenced by material conditions. The spiritual law is such that it will never lead you astray. If you follow spiritual law you cannot go wrong, but you need to have the courage to hold fast to a decision in favour of spiritual law.

3

In world affairs the individual work may turn the scale, may turn the affairs of humankind from evil to good. Good comes out of evil or ignorance. Good will come but you must know this truth in your hearts and minds. Your thoughts must dwell upon it; your speech must express this divine truth. You must live in the Star, and however contrary the conditions of earth may be, never give way to pessimism; never in any situation. Be sure that if you think aright, think creatively and positively, you are an instrument of God, for you set into operation the law of divine love, and the results will be wholly good. This is the form which true healing takes. Do you not see that when you can be kind and loving and helpful on every occasion—not in the hope of reward but because you cannot be happy unless you continually give forth the love of God—then, my brother, my sister, will you be a true healer; one walking amongst the masses radiating light—a true son/daughter of the Father-Mother God. Deep within your heart is the never-ending spring of life and power.

As you can live in this life and light, you are a brother of the light, and cannot fail in your efforts to help humankind. Do all you can, not to preach, but to live the gospel, to sow light in darkness, to sow goodness where there is lack of goodness; through love and 'God-thought' to stimulate the good in your brethren. Try to distinguish between the limitations of personality and the limitlessness of God's life. Live to send out light and this means seeing good in everything. If it doesn't appear to be good, then make it good. It will become good and will come right if you centre your vision upon God, because God is ever evolving, creating, bringing good out of evil, order out of chaos, light out of darkness. Guard well your thoughts, keep them pure in the love of God. The Master looks to the heart, for he knows that what is seen in the heart will be expressed in the thought, and what is expressed in the thought becomes a reality on the physical plane.

4

Dwell on beauty. Do not dwell on what appears to be ugly. Whatsoever things are lovely, true and good, think on these things. Let your ideal be of spotless purity held in the love and the wisdom of your Creator. Let your vision be of heaven. Think always of others in tenderness and understanding, not of yourself and your own desires. Keep within your heart the sweetness of the heavenly life. We all need patience, one with the other; therefore be patient with those around you, be good in thought towards your fellows. This is the way to develop your awareness of the invisible worlds, and the heavenly states of life. Give yourselves to purity and love so that you may be rightly guided and steered along life's pathway. It may not be easy for you at times, but God's messengers work, under divine law, to help you at every difficult corner, and as you journey onwards you will gain added strength, vision and light. Each one as an individual can start at this very minute to reflect that same glorious light. Surrender to divine wisdom, knowing that what is happening to you is a gift, an opportunity to grow in love, to draw closer to divine love. Do not think of life in the physical body as being the only life. Think of life as being eternal, and of yourself as a tiny spark of that divine life, one day to return to the heart of the Sun. Look up to the golden light of the Sun...... absorb into your being the golden rays......   In the silence of your own soul, kneel beside the still waters and pray to be able to send forth the healing light of the Son of God, the Christ. Behind you is a power beyond your comprehension, waiting only for Its children to be channels. May the channel open wide and the light flood through you to heal the whole world and raise it from death and darkness into everlasting light and glory.

5

Healing is a most beautiful work, because when you give yourselves for healing you are helping the spirit healers and God's angels to raise the consciousness of the masses of souls who suffer because they are in the dark. All humankind suffers from its ignorance and it is the work of the healing angels and all healers to illumine the consciousness. When you have dedicated yourselves to the healing work, do not limit your work by dwelling on sick physical bodies only, for that is but one form of healing. We would remind you that souls—the soul of the whole world needs healing—and the souls of men and women living on earth are sometimes brought into the presence of the Great Healer to be illumined spiritually, to be healed of their stresses, their sickness and their sadness. We would like every healer to know that you, as an individual, are part of a group, and what you do affects the whole of your particular group, not only the group with which you are working on earth, but also the heavenly group. Your world has yet to learn the happiness which God has designed for you, and this happiness can only come with true brotherhood, the brotherhood of the spirit.

The first step on the way to the realisation of this brotherhood is for every soul to learn to follow the inward light which teaches him or her to recognise the same light in every soul. We behind the veil say: 'follow the light within your own breast; obey the inner voice and you will never fail in brotherhood one to the other'. We would have you do likewise in your life. Go about the earth being love, being brotherly, not only to those who are congenial to you, but to all. Do not fall into the error of regarding anyone as your enemy. None is your enemy; all are your teachers. If you learn from another, be very glad to say 'Thank you, brother.' This is a wise attitude of mind. It is our work continually to express love, not to condemn, not to resent, not to fear, but to live peacefully, knowing that all moves forward to the desired culmination. The acts of a brother rise from the spirit. And so, in the days ahead, we ask you to walk continually in the consciousness of the Brotherhood unseen, of your individual guide as well as the great company of shining ones, who dwell for evermore in the consciousness of the light of Christ, in the peace and happiness of the Christ-life. The light of the Star, the light of Christ, can and will dispel the darkness on the earth and surrounding the earth. Those who know the way to give forth this light, continually give it forth with love and strength.

V. The Source Of All Healing

Love is the life within everything : the basis of all healing is love.

1

There are many methods of healing but there is only one true source from which healing flows. This source is the foundation of life, of love. This is the secret of all healing and to those who ask to learn how to heal, we say learn to love—love. Feel love in your heart towards God first, then to life and to nature.

Cultivate love, compassion, sympathy. Acknowledge that life is governed by law, and that law is God's law. It is when humankind separates itself from God's law that suffering enters in. If you experience what feel like 'crosses' in your life and in your work, hold fast to the simple feeling of love. This love will then flow through all areas of your life bringing transformation, and sometimes miracles! Seek first the wisdom and the love of God, then the power of healing will be generated and will flow into you. Kneel inwardly and worship the Source of your being. Know that when you aspire and pray to the Great Spirit, you will be enveloped and penetrated by a vibrant power, a divine energy, which will pour into your heart like the sun pouring through clouds. You will be bathed in this golden light, energised by the rays of the Sun, and at the same time offered the deep and eternal peace which comes from the knowledge of God's love and surrender to God's law.

2

The Master Jesus is the head of the healing ray. It is his special work to help humanity to reach contact with the Source of life. He comes to you whenever you truly call. Ordinary prayer is just an asking for something for self, or for someone else. No true prayer ever goes unanswered because it sets up a vibration in the soul which goes right to the Source of supply. But it must be true, sincere prayer, and there must be complete surrender of the soul to God's will. Then we assure you that the magical healing power will work. It is not just a fantasy; it is a working proposition. If you do your best to put love into operation in yourself, in your own life, and turn to the Source of life within your being, always endeavouring to surrender to God's will, miracles can and will happen. You will remember that Jesus said on a number of occasions before he performed a miracle of healing, *'I and my Father are one'*. This is the secret, 'I and my Father are one'. You as individual brethren are all learning that you are part of, that you are one with the Great Spirit, with the

Father-Mother God. You breathe with, your heart beats with Him-Her, God. We would suggest to every would-be healer, that you practise this meditation whenever you have the opportunity. Long words are not necessary. Repeat over and over: 'Father-Mother, we are one... we are one in You. We are one.' As you practise this affirmation/meditation you will develop your ability to receive and project the God-power, the Christ-power. We on our side of life see how much is built by prayers and aspirations. We see a beam of light, a channel of light which appears to be like a 'v' shape. Into this channel which is opened through an individual soul's humble aspiration, there flows heavenly light, guidance and wisdom... and all the help that is needed. The powers of the Divine work slowly, but perfectly harmoniously. If an earnest prayer is sent forth, there is always an answer. Someone is always used in some way to answer a prayer of the heart. There is a perfect heavenly plan in operation. No prayer is left unanswered. Go forward quietly, and when you least expect it, the light will burst upon your pathway and your vision will become clearer. Try to feel that you are one tiny spark of the blazing light. Feel that you are in it, you are breathing, thinking, working, in this eternal life and love.

3

The basis of all healing, as the Great Healer himself said, is love. He simply said: *'Love one another'*. That is all. This love in the human heart—compassion, understanding, love—this it is which is the power of the white magic, the power of the Christ, the power which heals. Since this love is light, it is the power of all healing. Light has many colours, and certain colours are selected for certain patients in your healing work, but all colours are light and originate from light. Light is born of God. Light is the love, the son-daughter of the Father-Mother, Creator of life. This light has been worshipped in the form of Jesus the Christ, and worshipped universally as the great light in the heavens, the light of the Sun. Long ago the mystic words went forth, 'Let there be Light!'. There is a vibration from the heart of God which radiates Light. When you have realised your union with that Light within your innermost being, you will understand the power of these words. Then you too will send forth a vibration into the denser ether interpenetrating the physical plane. Such sending forth from your broadcasting house is more potent than any action.

4

Were it not for sunlight, which is both physical and spiritual in its essence, life could not exist. The earth itself is imbued with these fires from the sun. Another word for this fire is 'love'. This love is the life within everything. So, were your vision clear, you would see the divine fire within even what are called inanimate things, such as metals, stones, wood, all are pulsating with tiny sparks of light and fire. All nature is also pulsating with these forces. If you could look upon a tree with your spiritual eyes, you would see far more than the trunk, branches and foliage of that tree. You would see the fire shining in the earth around its roots, and rising as sap to pulsate through every section of that tree, radiating light everywhere.

For this divine fire shines not only in the sky but everywhere, in the earth itself and in all nature. This earth is not dark and solid as may be supposed, but a star of light. In the same way the spirit of humankind, when it is developed, emits, not only a spiritual light visible to the clairvoyant, but an actual physical light. In the body of a Master this light can be seen shining forth. This is not imagination; it is fact. What can be done by a Master, can be done by you also, in time, in time. To those of you who are already, or who wish to be spiritual healers, we would say that the first essential is to get attunement between your innermost thought and aspiration and the great spirit of Christ. Aspire to become united with the cosmic Light, and to feel that light pouring into you. Learn to send forth continually, not from your lips but from within your innermost being, light... love! The light blazes in the heavens; the light blazes unseen within physical matter. We would have you never forget the ever-present light, and we would remind you again of the power of those words: I am the resurrection and the life. As you meditate on those words you will understand more and more of the meaning, and you will realise the warm glow of the light and the power which rises up in you, bidden to rise by the God within your heart.

5

We give you a sacred charge. Maybe some will feel unready. But trust that this now is the right moment for you. Each individual soul can make an effort to start to understand what is meant by the inner light. Each individual soul can give itself in service to humanity. Service on the outer plane is of value; service on the inner planes, in the silence, is of greater value still. You can serve humanity in no better way than this, by becoming an instrument for the forces of the light. There is no limit to the rays of light which can pour through you and extend over the whole earth. If you could see from our side of life you would see great rays of light like searchlights going out when groups meet together to send out the light. You would see rays like searchlights in the sky going out from all over the world. Even in your loneliness you can work to send out this beautiful and true Light, the Christ Light, the Christ love. We are teaching you to direct it with purpose and with knowledge. We would point out to you also, very gently, the way to recognise and distinguish the true light from the false. This is so necessary when the spirit is in the body of flesh, because always there is the pull of the body; there is domination by the earthly mind, and the voice of the earthly mind can so easily be mistaken for the voice of the spirit, the true light. The true light is not dominating. The soul which is guided by the true light thinks not of itself; the self is forgotten in thought for others. If your voice urges you to act in a selfish way you can be sure that it is a false message. The true light is a gentle love which rises in you causing you to look out on the world with understanding and with respect. Remember that respect. When you respect the soul of your brother/sister you respect his/her life in every way. There is not nearly enough respect one for another! This is a quality which must be brought forth in a would-be healer, this respect, this gentle spirit of understanding flowing from one to another.

If the Star is in you, and you are radiating that light, you are helping all creatures.

We in the world of spirit would weld you closer together! We would unite you heart to heart, so that you work as a great Star of light. When you visualise the Star and send it forth, you are sending out pure light into the world. You are truly healing the world. At every service held in the White Eagle Lodge you are asked to project the six-pointed Star by the power of thought. This star is indicative of the divine Light, the Christ Light. When you are concentrating on the blazing Star, the Christ Star, it illumines the whole atmosphere, the whole ether. We remind you once again of the power of the star to help all humankind and the very earth itself. Nothing but good is accomplished by your linking with the star. Train yourself to concentrate upon that symbol of the Christ-life, the shining six-pointed Star, for it will guide you, unfailingly, to the place of perfect healing. When in doubt, when in need, always look up to that Star. Visualise it shining above you, its rays pouring down into your head and heart, and surrounding you in an aura of light. Of yourself you can do nothing, but you can be an instrument for this healing light of the Christ Star. By holding the thought of the Star in your heart, you are always working for your fellow creatures. You cannot do otherwise. The light of the star will turn all darkness into light: light will absorb all the darkness.

7

When you wish to send out healing light from the Christ Star, just think of God and love and see the object or person that you wish to help within the star. You do not need to work hard mentally: just love. To send out the Star, be kind, not critical. Do not be critical, be kind and loving, uniting your soul with the cosmic life. Say to yourself, 'the Father and I are one…. the Father and we are all one'. So the Star is built and the light floods from you and from the simple united company of brethren on earth and in the world of light. Think of this when you are sending out your Star. Be constant and steadfast, looking at all times into the light of the Christ star. When you are working alone, as some of you must, and when you are working as a group, as some of you continually do, keep your soul steady and create in your soul-vision a Star without limitation. Whatever your personal need, you will gain comfort and strength and peace of soul by continually creating and beholding this ever-shining star in the ether. The Star is not only a great cosmic power, it is also a tender, loving, guiding power, a protecting power in your own lives. If you can surrender yourselves to the sweet and lovely Star radiance, you will find that your pathway will be one of light and happiness and gentle peace. Do not falter on your way; keep your vision upon the Star and remember that you are serving mankind by your courage and steadfastness, and you can serve your own cause as you serve the cause of brotherhood and the coming of the light onto the earth, the physical plane.

8

There is so much for you all to learn about the divine magic which lies in the heart of the Star. Never doubt that the Star is permeating the whole of your physical life. It represents the Christ power and the Christ love in human life. Send forth the light of the Star everywhere with love and kindness; never forcing, but gently sunning and watering the seed in the heart of mankind. Think what the effect would be if millions in the world were thus radiating light. Think what the effect would be if humans abandoned thoughts of self, desire for accumulation or protection for self, and held fast to one dominating thought of peace and brotherhood, and to help men and women to the way of Christ. If the Star is in your thoughts, if you think of the meaning of the Star, then you become a creator for the Star. If you hold in your mind the symbol of the Star and if you project that Star to any situation that is inharmonious, or shall we say immature, you will be used as an instrument to bring about harmony and right thinking and right action in others. You send out the light and you pray for your own country, and for others, and the Brotherhood would tell you that all the world needs your light, your love. Persevere with your work and you will see the slow but definite effect of the star upon the leaders of all nations. You will see the slow but steady shooting from the dark earth of materialism of the little plants of green, which are little rays of light. For as nature works slowly, so does the spiritual life grow and unfold slowly and imperceptibly. Hold this thought steadily without a break. Pray that you may hold steadily to the thought of the power of God, the Christ power, the Christ light. Will you make this effort? For we tell you that the hosts of heaven are ready and waiting to help 'you'. The light of Christ will save humankind; this spirit alone will be the saviour of the world.

VI. A Healing Blessing

Develop the spirit within you—and assist in the spiritualisation of all life.

1

Remember, in the healing work, that quite apart from healing the physical body, you are doing something even more important. You are helping in the building of a most beautiful house of God — the temple of God — the individual. You are not only smoothing away pain, and healing the inharmony of the body, but you are also helping in the strengthening and the spiritualisation of the individual. What a glorious work, and how necessary it is for all healers to concentrate upon the spiritualisation of their own consciousness, and the spiritualisation of all life! This is why naturally healers endeavour to purify their own temple. Imagine a perfect healing temple, and if you will see it, visualise it, you will feel the glory of the life here in spirit. It is for you, it is part of you. The purpose of your incarnation is for you to become stronger and stronger in spiritual light and power so that you may bring through into daily life the radiance of your spiritual life.

Nothing matters more than this spiritual life in you. It is the key into heaven: heaven on earth as well as the heaven world after death. Spiritual powers have no limit. With psychic powers you are depending upon certain conditions of the human body, of the human life, but with the development of spiritual gifts your power to penetrate the unseen realms becomes unlimited.

2

Psychic gifts are useful, but remember that they will only penetrate the psychic planes immediately surrounding the earth. Those of you who would develop your gifts of true spiritual clairvoyance need to seek the inner mystery of your own being. Try to open yourselves to the higher mind, to the celestial mind, and what will be revealed to you will not be imagination; it will be truth. All need to learn this truth in the course of incarnation.

You may think that only in spirit, away from earth conditions, will you learn profound cosmic truth, but it is whilst you are in a physical body that you learn that you are spirit; that you live and have your being in the Great Spirit; and that behind you is a power, a life force, which is your strength, your guide, your help. Cut yourself off from the darkness and the ignorance of the earthly life. Rise into that higher self, and you will instantly feel the inflow of the life force, the healing power, the wisdom, the love and the strength, the joy and peace, which come from God. Withdraw each day from the tumult of the outer world, and try to feel the presence of your noble heavenly self. Look to that self for your guidance and your inspiration in life. Try to be strong and poised and true to that enduring self.

3

We remind you that there are two aspects of your life. You know this, but we want to emphasise it for you. Unfortunately some people think that the personality they know on this physical plane is all of them; but remember that only a very small part of you is imprisoned in physical life. What is manifesting through the body is only the point of the triangle. God has given you the power to realise and contact your higher self. Every day on waking and many times during the day, particularly when you are being overwhelmed by the affairs of the physical life, pause and remember that it is the little self, the human personality which is being tried, and then understand that above you in the invisible realms is that greater self, the Christself. Look into that form of glorious colour, that radiant life, and you will feel infinite power flowing into your personality. You will be conscious, above your personality, of a self which is limitless, which is living in God; and in this higher self you can meet and commune with your elder brethren, indeed with all brethren with whom you long to work for the spiritual progress of all humanity. Only in the little self are separation and fear known. Rise above the little self, and so become enfolded by the love of God, of spirit. By loving and by obeying the commands of the Great Spirit of love you set in motion those spiritual forces which attune your innermost consciousness to the Source of all being, and you receive into your innermost, streams of light and power from Christ, who is all love and light. In the silence deep within your heart you will become aware of the love of God, and of the love and wisdom of those great ones who live and work for their younger brethren. May you be raised above the smallness of the little self, and hold communion with the Great, the universal Spirit, God.

4

Men and women will come to know in this new age that they are spirit, pure spirit; and that they have been given certain vehicles or bodies in order to bring through into outer manifestation a very beautiful quality of love. This is the purpose of life on earth. When you meditate on this truth, you will realise its profundity and what it could mean to every living creature. We believe, surely we believe, that the Great Spirit, who is watching over all human children, has given them this greatest gift, the seed within the human heart, the seed of love. Eye hath not seen nor ear heard the glories, the beauties which are prepared for you, for everyone in the kingdom of pure, divine love. In the age of Aquarius upon which the world is entering, you will see a great advance in mental and in spiritual growth! Both go hand-in-hand. The new age is bringing to men and woman higher knowledge, including great knowledge of healing. The veil between the world of matter and the world of spirit will be removed, and there will be established true communion of spirit. Death will be swallowed up in the victory of the Christ Spirit becoming triumphant in human life. Many grumblers think that a golden age is just a dream. But dreams, as we very well know and can speak from experience, eventually create external conditions. Without vision the people perish! So hold your dreams and keep on keeping on. So many cannot do this; they go to sleep by the wayside. They get discouraged; they turn back; they go down a little slope, and sleep. But the soul who perseveres and keeps on keeping on, reaches the goal of spiritual liberation.

5

You will often hear of the symbol of the lily being given by spiritual teachers or shown in meditation. The lily shown on the surface of water is an ancient symbol of the unfolding of spiritual gifts. This is why we have told some of you who desire to cultivate gifts of the spirit, first to close your eyes and ears to all that is physical around you, and to create a vision in your mind of harmonious, beautiful sunlit gardens, where you may see flowers in profusion. We have suggested you walk in thought through the gardens until you come to a fountain of light. Then to visualise this fountain of sparkling light; go right under it and let the sparks of light pour over you and recharge you. Breathe in slowly and steadily...... Breathe out...... Keep on breathing in this light. Now every atom of your body is charged with this light, which is perfect life. Now walk through the gardens to the innermost sanctuary, passing through the gate which is wide open... and within that inner temple, see the silent water, pure and still and so clear. The still water of the spirit is clear as crystal. You may look into that water, and see the reflection of yourself, for the waters of the spirit never lie. On the surface of the water you will see the water lily, pure white, with a centre of gold, white and gold, symbolical of purity, and divine intelligence. Rest quietly in contemplation of this perfect flower.

6

Can you visualise again now a temple of the Star Brotherhood, filled with countless white-robed brethren, praising their Creator? Can you hear the music of the spheres of light, and realise that every incident in the human lives of these white-robed brethren has gone to create this heavenly music? They have suffered; they have known joy and pain, even as you on earth know joy and pain. But the joy and pain of human life are threads used to weave the wedding garment of the spirit, without which no soul can enter into the heaven world. These numberless souls seen in this vision, who make up the grand company of heaven, have passed through the tribulation of earthly sorrows and joys, without which suffering they could not have woven the garment which made them eligible for the heavenly state of life. Kneeling round the altar in the Temple of the Star, with hands together, uplifted, they are worshipping the ever-growing light of the jewel within the lotus. Daily, in your meditations seek this jewel in the heart of the lotus, for here you will find all wisdom. You will learn to go direct to the jewel and with tender heart, with the mind of the heart, you will comprehend truth. You will know nothing and everything. You will think with the heart-mind, with the intuition. Always look within. The flash of intuition will be like the spoken word to you, God's voice, telling you truth. Judge not that ye be not judged. If you continually look into the gentle love of the Christ-heart you will judge no-one but yourself. May this meditation and these words inspire you, and lead you forward on your path to become a true healer.

7

The Brotherhood of the Star bring you love, bring you blessing, blessing upon your work. Every human and spiritual need will be met when you seek the gentle heart of Christ. Whenever you would heal, first of all seek the communion table. . . . make that contact from your heart chakra with the Son, with the Great Healer, and, as you do so, breathing in the life and light of your Creator, you are filled, filled with that miraculous healing power which will pour through you. This is the power of love. The power of love works miracles in your life. Divine love will meet every human need......

We would leave you with a sense of deep security and peace. Focus your thoughts, place your trust in God. Let nothing disturb you, attune yourself to all-good...... to God. Put your hand in the hand of the divine Son, even Christ, and no inharmony can touch you, nothing can hurt you. This is eternal truth. Peace be in your hearts. Search for true wisdom of the spirit, the wisdom which perceives the law of God working through life; which discriminates between the things which matter, the real; and the unreal and transient, which tomorrow pass into the unknown.

May the peace of the eternal stillness, the tranquillity of spirit abide with you in all your ways. May joy fill your heart and spirit now and for evermore. God bless you all.

Amen. Amen. Amen.

HEAL THYSELF

White Eagle

YOUR KEY TO SPIRITUAL HEALING AND HEALTH
IN MIND AND BODY

The higher self of each of us, which we can learn
to contact, knows no limitation. The Christ
healing and radiance flows through our higher self
and can melt away all ills and resolve all difficulties.
This book shows a way for everyone to find and
retain true health of mind and body.

62 + xviii pp, paperback, 18.6 x 12.3 cm
ISBN 978-0-85497-107-0
Double CD also available
ISBN 978-0-85497-148-3

SEEKING SERENITY

White Eagle

FINDING FREEDOM FROM FEAR

White Eagle shows how awareness of a higher world, from which love flows, can bring infinite comfort to every soul. 'Train yourself in the way of serenity', he says—and shows us how to do so.

83 + xiii pp, paperback, 198 x 129 mm
ISBN 978-0-85487-184-1

PRACTISING PEACE

White Eagle

A new edition of the book
THE GENTLE BROTHER

'The light of the spirit can shine from your heart, from your whole body. The heart centre can be like a lighted torch on a dark night, and can cast a beam into darkened highways. This is the very light of the universe, the true light of God, the dynamic force which can perform miracles.'

71 + ix pp, paperback, 186 x 123 mm
ISBN 978-0-85487-185-8

LIVING WITH LOVE

White Eagle

A new edition of the book
GOLDEN HARVEST

'Within you is the golden light of the sun, and only you can release this radiation from within your own centre. Try to realize that within your heart is the same blazing, golden Sun as the one you contemplate in your meditations, and that this infinite source of power is within your own being.'

70 + x pp, paperback, 186 x 123 mm
ISBN 978-0-85487-186-5

THE WHITE EAGLE PUBLISHING TRUST, which publishes and distributes the White Eagle teaching, is part of the wider work of the White Eagle Lodge, a 'wisdom school' for the present age, in which people may find a place for growth and understanding, and where the teachings of White Eagle find practical expression. Here men and women may come to learn the reason for their life on earth and how to serve and live in harmony with the whole brotherhood of life, visible and invisible, in health and happiness. The White Eagle Publishing Trust website is at:

www.whiteaglepublishing.org

For readers wishing to know more of the work of The White Eagle Lodge visit our websites at:

www.whiteagle.org (worldwide)
www.whiteaglelodge.org (Americas)
www.whiteeaglelodge.org.au (Australasia)
www.whiteagleca.com (Canada)

and you can email us at the addresses

enquiries@whiteagle.org (worldwide)
sjrc@whiteaglelodge.org (Americas), and
enquiries@whiteeaglelodge.org.au (Australasia)

or alternatively write to The White Eagle Lodge, New Lands, Brewells Lane, Liss, Hampshire, England GU33 7HY (tel: 01739 893300). In the Americas to The Church of the White Eagle Lodge, P.O. Box 930, Montgomery, Texas 77356 (tel: 936-597 5757), and in Australasia to The White Eagle Lodge (Australasia), P.O. Box 225, Maleny, Queensland 4552, Australia (tel: 07 5494 4169).